Pioneers on Land

by Alex Hall

Minneapolis, Minnesota

Credits
Images are courtesy of Shutterstock.com. With thanks to Getty Images, Thinkstock Photo, and iStockphoto. Recurring images – Dancake. Cover – Rudra Narayan Mitra, Vixit, Dancake. 4–5 – Charles Knowles, Winston Springwater. 6–7 – Salviati, Public domain, via Wikimedia Commons, saisnaps. 8–9 – Edgar Samuel Paxson, Public domain, via Wikimedia Commons, Dsdugan, CC0, via Wikimedia Commons. 10–11 – Tracy Grazley, Ace Diamond. 12–13 – Everett Collection. 14–15 – H. J. Myers, photographer, Public domain, via Wikimedia Commons, ALEXEY GRIGOREV. 16–17 – Wm. Notman and Son, Public domain, via Wikimedia Commons, Johnston, John S., Public domain, via Wikimedia Commons, Melnikov Dmitriy, Unknown author, collection of the Museum of the City of New York via Wikimedia Commons. 18–19 – picture copied from the Gertrude Bell Archive [1], Public domain, via Wikimedia Commons, Jakl Lubos. 20–21 – Studio Tourne, Public domain, via Wikimedia Commons, KathySG. 22–23 – William J. Root, Chicago, Public domain, via Wikimedia Commons, Regina M art. 24–25 – AnonymousUnknown author, Public domain, via Wikimedia Commons, bilinmiyor, CC BY-SA 4.0 <https://creativecommons.org/licenses/by-sa/4.0>, via Wikimedia Commons. 26–27 – Jamling Tenzing Norgay, CC BY-SA 3.0 <https://creativecommons.org/licenses/by-sa/3.0>, via Wikimedia Commons, Vixit. 28–29 – Sergey Goryachev. 30 – solarseven.

Bearport Publishing Company Product Development Team
Publisher: Jen Jenson; Director of Product Development: Spencer Brinker; Managing Editor: Allison Juda; Editor: Cole Nelson; Associate Editor: Naomi Reich; Associate Editor: Tiana Tran; Art Director: Colin O'Dea; Designer: Kim Jones; Designer: Kayla Eggert; Product Development Specialist: Owen Hamlin

Library of Congress Cataloging-in-Publication Data is available at www.loc.gov or upon request from the publisher.

ISBN: 979-8-89232-877-7 (hardcover)
ISBN: 979-8-89232-963-7 (paperback)
ISBN: 979-8-89232-907-1 (ebook)

© 2025 BookLife Publishing
This edition is published by arrangement with BookLife Publishing.

North American adaptations © 2025 Bearport Publishing Company. All rights reserved. No part of this publication may be reproduced in whole or in part, stored in any retrieval system, or transmitted in any form or by any means, electronic, mechanical, photocopying, recording, or otherwise, without written permission from the publisher.

For more information, write to Bearport Publishing, 5357 Penn Avenue South, Minneapolis, MN 55419.

CONTENTS

Your Journey on Land 4
Marco Polo 6
Sacagawea 8
David Livingstone 12
Nellie Bly 14
Gertrude Bell 18
Annie Londonderry 20
Roald Amundsen 24
Edmund Hillary and Tenzing Norgay 26
Where Will a Journey on Land Take You? . . 30
Glossary 31
Index 32
Read More 32
Learn More Online 32

Your Journey on Land

Welcome, adventurers! We are going to follow the paths of some amazing pioneers on land.

Many explorers have traveled through forests, across deserts, and up mountains to learn more about the world.

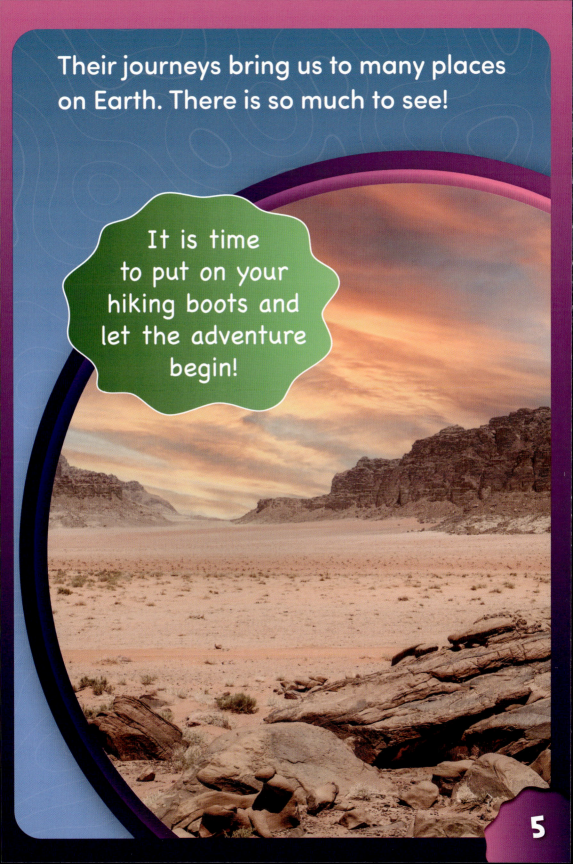

Their journeys bring us to many places on Earth. There is so much to see!

It is time to put on your hiking boots and let the adventure begin!

MARCO POLO

AROUND 1254–1324

Our journey starts in Italy with a man named Marco Polo. He left his home to explore with his father and uncle. They traveled to China.

Marco wanted to learn about China. The **emperor** of China wanted to learn about Europe.

The emperor gave Marco a golden passport that let him travel all over China. Marco made many of his trips riding camels.

Marco wrote a book about his adventures. Many people were amazed by his stories about life in China.

SACAGAWEA
AROUND 1788–AROUND 1812

Let's travel across the United States. We are following Sacagawea, a Native American woman of the Shoshone **tribe**.

Sacagawea became an **interpreter** for some explorers on an **expedition** across North America. Meriwether Lewis and William Clark led the group.

When Sacagawea joined the expedition, she had just had a baby. She cared for her young son throughout the journey.

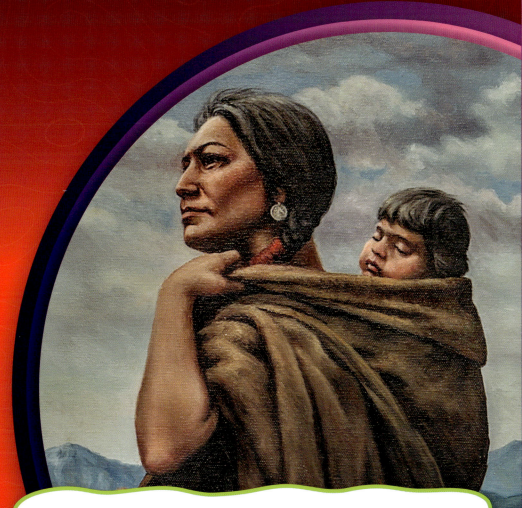

One of the things Sacagawea did was help the group find food. She knew which plants were safe to eat.

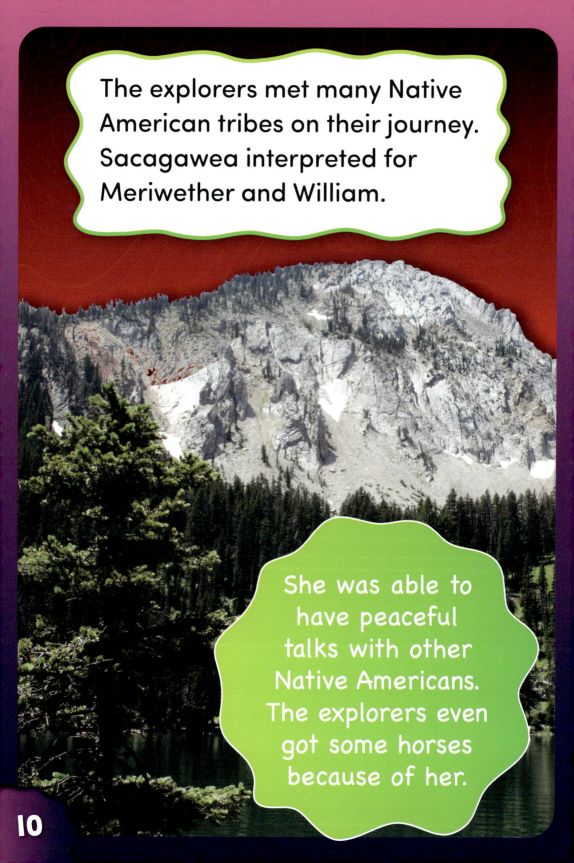

The explorers met many Native American tribes on their journey. Sacagawea interpreted for Meriwether and William.

She was able to have peaceful talks with other Native Americans. The explorers even got some horses because of her.

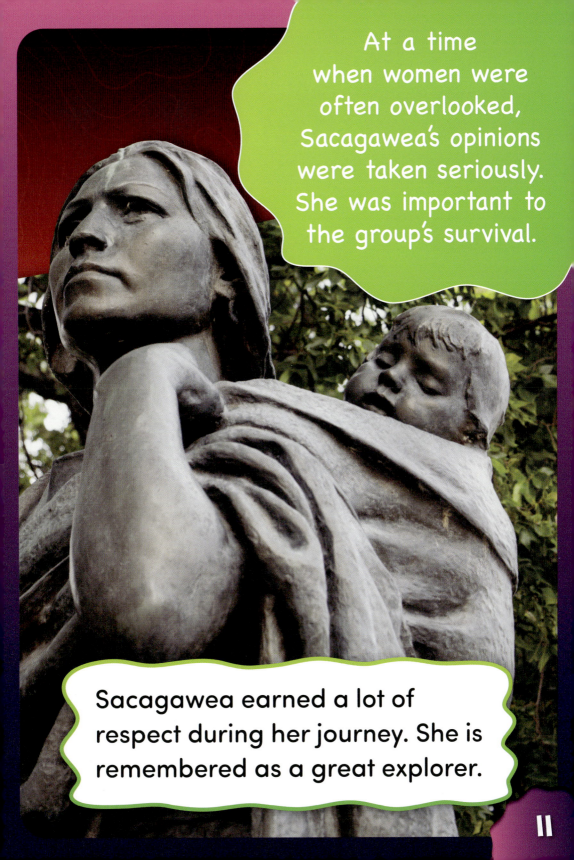

At a time when women were often overlooked, Sacagawea's opinions were taken seriously. She was important to the group's survival.

Sacagawea earned a lot of respect during her journey. She is remembered as a great explorer.

DAVID LIVINGSTONE

1813–1873

Our next adventurer is Scottish doctor David Livingstone.

He spent many years exploring Africa. He became famous for stories of his travels.

During one journey, David disappeared. He had been searching for the start of the Nile, one of the world's longest rivers. He was eventually found alive.

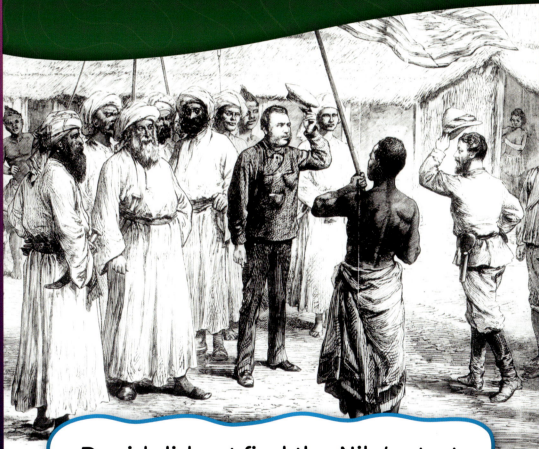

David did not find the Nile's start. However, he met many people and made other discoveries during his adventures.

NELLIE BLY
1864–1922

Nellie Bly was born in Pennsylvania. However, her biggest adventure began in New Jersey.

Nellie was a journalist. Her job was to write about what was happening in the world.

She read a made-up story about a character who traveled around the world in 80 days. Nellie believed she could beat that time.

Some people thought this trip would be impossible for a woman to complete. Nellie knew they were wrong.

Nellie set out on her journey. She rode trains, ships, and even donkeys.

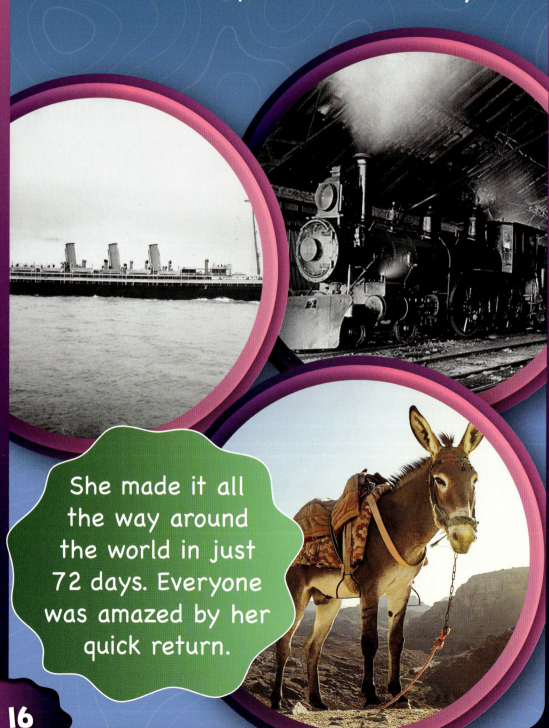

She made it all the way around the world in just 72 days. Everyone was amazed by her quick return.

Nellie became famous because of her trip. She wrote a book about her adventure around the world.

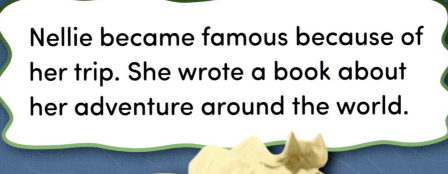

Nellie's **determination** helped her make history.

GERTRUDE BELL
1868–1926

If you want to see a fearless adventurer, then let's follow English explorer Gertrude Bell!

Gertrude climbed many mountains in the Swiss Alps. One of the mountain peaks was later named after her.

During one climb, Gertrude got **frostbite**. This did not stop her love for climbing. Just two years later, she went up a mountain named Matterhorn.

Gertrude always looked for new adventures. She achieved many amazing things.

MATTERHORN

19

ANNIE LONDONDERRY

1870–1947

Annie Londonderry was born in Latvia. She moved to the United States at a young age. When she was about 23, she decided to ride a bicycle around the world.

No woman had ever done something like this before, but that did not stop Annie.

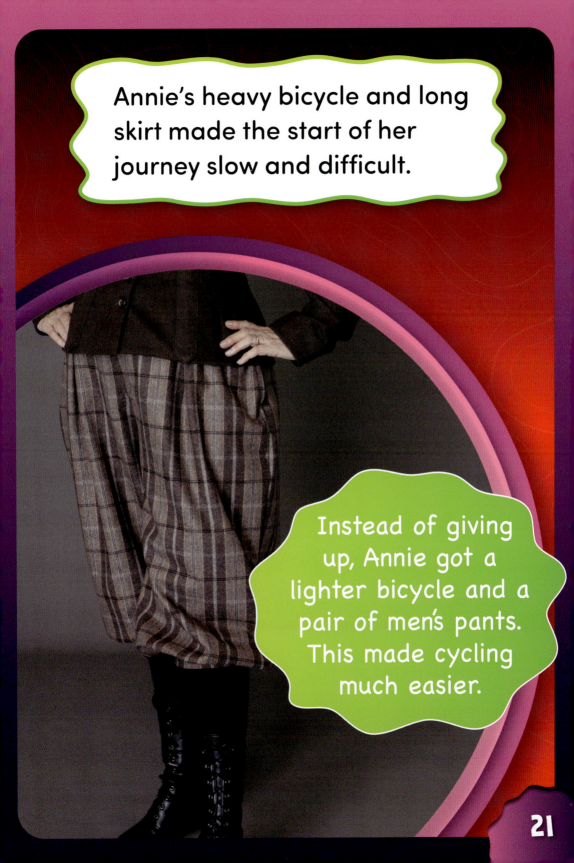

Annie's heavy bicycle and long skirt made the start of her journey slow and difficult.

Instead of giving up, Annie got a lighter bicycle and a pair of men's pants. This made cycling much easier.

During the ride, Annie had a bad fall and broke her arm. But she kept going.

She completed her journey in just under 15 months. Annie was the first woman to ride a bicycle around the world.

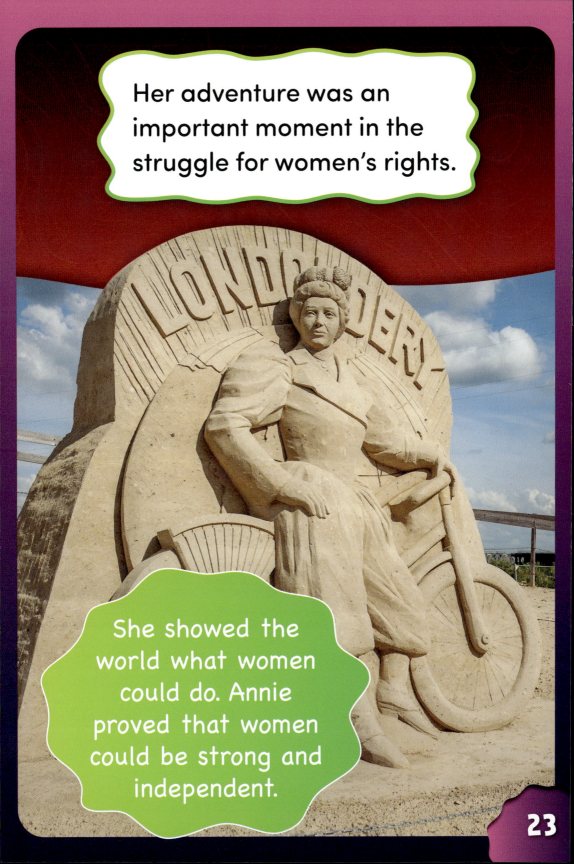

Her adventure was an important moment in the struggle for women's rights.

She showed the world what women could do. Annie proved that women could be strong and independent.

ROALD AMUNDSEN

1872–1928

It is time to head to the most southern place on Earth. A Norwegian man named Roald Amundsen wanted to reach the South Pole in Antarctica.

Others had tried before him, but the cold and snow made the journey too difficult.

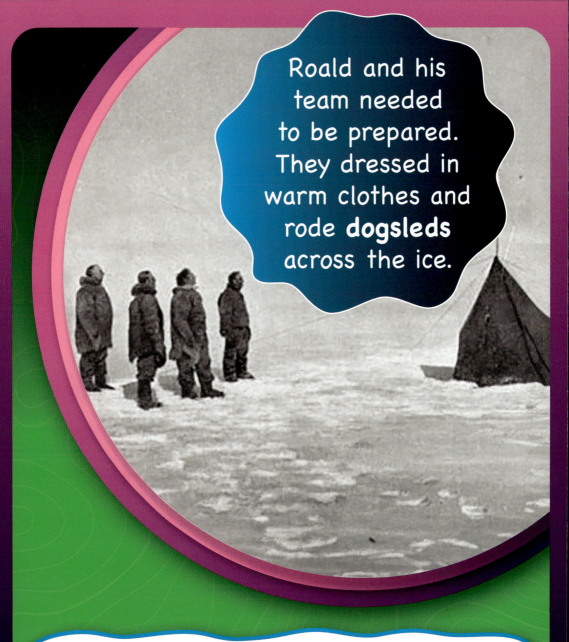

Roald and his team needed to be prepared. They dressed in warm clothes and rode **dogsleds** across the ice.

These explorers were the first to reach the South Pole. Roald's careful planning made the journey successful.

25

EDMUND HILLARY AND TENZING NORGAY

Edmund Hillary was a climber from New Zealand. Tenzing Norgay was a **Sherpa** from Nepal. They both wanted to climb Mount Everest in the Himalayas.

EDMUND HILLARY

1919–2008

Bad weather and thin air make Everest very difficult to climb.

TENZING NORGAY

1914–1986

Many other people had failed to reach the top. Edmund and Tenzing decided to work together to climb to Earth's highest point.

MOUNT EVEREST

Just three days after another team gave up, Edmund and Tenzing began to climb the mountain.

This was Edmund's fourth Himalayan expedition in about two years. It was Tenzing's seventh attempt to climb Everest. Their experience made them a great team.

The pair used air tanks to help them breathe during the climb.

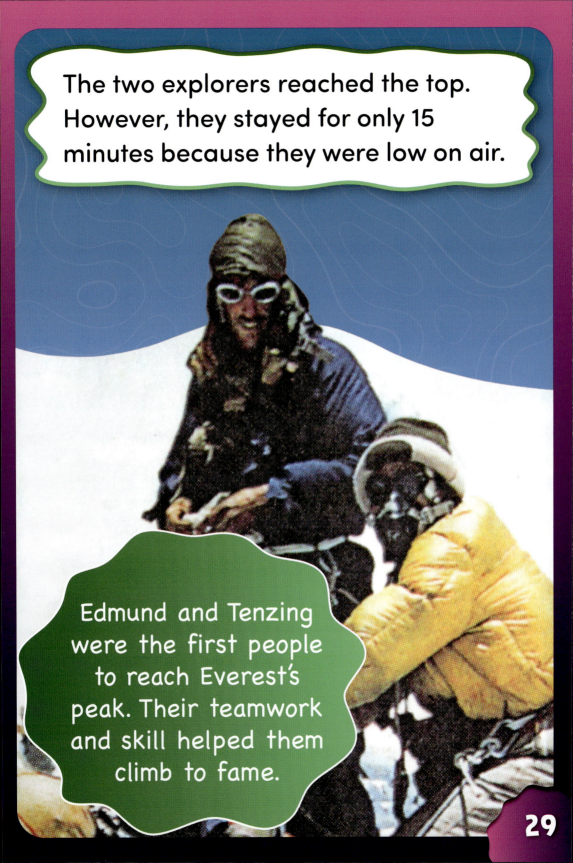

The two explorers reached the top. However, they stayed for only 15 minutes because they were low on air.

Edmund and Tenzing were the first people to reach Everest's peak. Their teamwork and skill helped them climb to fame.

WHERE WILL A JOURNEY ON LAND TAKE YOU?

Exploring the world is exciting! There is still so much to discover.

Would you like to lead the next journey on land? People may talk about your amazing adventures!

GLOSSARY

determination a strong will to do something

dogsleds small, flat sleds pulled by groups of dogs

emperor a person who rules over an area of land and its people

expedition a long trip taken for a specific purpose

frostbite damage to part of the body due to extreme cold

interpreter someone who explains what things mean between different languages

Sherpa a person who is from a group in the Himalaya mountains that is known for helping other mountain climbers

tribe a group of people who live together

INDEX

bicycle 20–22
book 7, 17
expedition 8–9, 28
mountain 4, 18–19, 27
pants 21
passport 7
river 13
Sherpa 26
Shoshone 8
South Pole 24–25

READ MORE

Marriott, Emma. *Explorapedia: Amazing Explorers of the World and Their Journeys of Discovery (Lonely Planet Kids).* Wilson, WY: Lonely Planet Global, 2022.

Rains, Dalton. *Lewis and Clark and Sacagawea (Explorations).* Mendota Heights, MN: Apex Editions, 2025.

LEARN MORE ONLINE

1. Go to **FactSurfer.com** or scan the QR code below.

2. Enter **"Pioneers on Land"** into the search box.

3. Click on the cover of this book to see a list of websites.